Philip Grushkin: *a retrospective*

THE GROLIER CLUB
NEW YORK
2001

Published to coincide with an exhibition held at
The Grolier Club
28 March through 25 May, 2001

PHILIP GRUSHKIN WAS A BOOKMAN.
His life was devoted to creating important and beautiful
books, and he engineered many of the very best. He was a book
designer, a calligrapher, a graphic artist, and a teacher of the
book arts. He lived his life surrounded by books and by book
people.

During his long career, he illustrated book jackets and
designed hundreds of books for distinguished publishers
including Harry N. Abrams, Abbeville, Alfred A. Knopf,
Random House, George Braziller, Harcourt Brace, World,
Prentice-Hall, David Godine, Aldo Sessa, Hugh Lauter Levin,
Limited Editions Club, and many others. For more than ten
years he was Art Director and Vice President at Abrams,
before founding his own company, Philip Grushkin, Inc.

He served as publishing consultant to the New York
Graphic Society, Rizzoli, Abbeville, Cosmogonias (Buenos
Aires, Argentina), and Ciba-Geigy. He was a long-standing
member of the Grolier Club, the Typophiles, the Society of
Scribes, AIGA, and the American Printing History
Association. He was a founding member of the Art Center of
Northern New Jersey.

Among the books he designed which are standard works
worldwide are:

THE HISTORY OF ART by H.W. Janson

THE HISTORY OF FAR EASTERN ART
    by Sherman Lee

THE ATLAS OF HUMAN ANATOMY by Frank H.
    Netter, MD

THE ART OF FLORENCE by Glenn Andres, John
    Hunisak, and A. Richard Turner

CELLINI by John Pope-Hennessy

A WORLD HISTORY OF PHOTOGRAPHY by
    Naomi Rosenblum

ROBERT MOSES: THE POWER BROKER
by Robert A. Caro

THE ART OF ROCK *by Paul D. Grushkin*

SELF-PORTRAIT: USA *by David Douglas Duncan*

Phil Grushkin was the most admired pupil of George Salter, one of America's greatest calligraphers and book designers. Like George, Phil became a renowned teacher, first at Cooper Union, then at Harvard/Radcliffe, and finally at New York University. Twice he accepted the Chinese government's invitation to teach book design in Beijing.

He lectured in Russia, Japan, Europe, and Argentina, and at the New York Public Library. He produced many memorable programs for the Heritage of the Graphic Arts series. His collection of bookmaking slides was legendary, and he carried his cameras — he was proudest of his Zeiss Contarex — around the globe.

He was a calligrapher, known for his beautiful Steuben Glass logo and the distinctive hand and air-brushed lettering he brought to hundreds of book jacket assignments. Among his fellow calligrapher friends, he is remembered for the delightful hand-drawn holiday greeting cards he and his wife Jean produced over many years. He also was a cartographer, first for the U.S. Geological Survey, and, during World War II, for the Office of Strategic Services (OSS).

Everyone he worked for, and worked with, marveled at his artistry. Publishers and authors alike were profoundly grateful for the intuitive and gentlemanly skills he brought to making books. Here is what some said of him:

from John Pope-Hennessy at the New York Metropolitan Museum of Art, in a personal letter:

> I received the first copy of Cellini yesterday and I want to say at once how superlatively well the trouble you took to design the book has paid off. It is beautifully designed, and I have found it a continuous pleasure both to turn the pages and to read it.

From Dr. Frank Netter, author of The Atlas of Human Anatomy, in the acknowledgements:

> I wish to express herewith my admiration for the artistry and skill of Mr. Philip Grushkin, who did the overall and

typographic designs, made the mechanicals, and oversaw the entire production and printing of this atlas. Its visual appeal, readability, and fine quality of pictorial reproduction are largely attributable to him, and his efficiency of operation greatly expedited its production.

H. W. Janson praised Phil's "admirable skill and patience." Naomi Rosenblum cited his "sensitivity and meticulousness." Sherman Lee thanked him for his "diligence and expert craftsmanship."

To what can we attribute this bookman's sensibility?

Philip Grushkin grew up in Brooklyn and upon completing high school was determined to find his peers among the centuries of fine art masters. By the end of his long and accomplished life, there was scarcely a painter, a sculptor, a typographer, or a calligrapher from whom he did not draw his inspiration.

What was the nature of this man's gift? In the view of many, it was Phil Grushkin's creative application of both fundamentals and intuitive technique which became the very essentials of this bookmaking engineer's bravado. In the words of Everette Fahy, writing from the Frick Collection, "Philip Grushkin's brilliant layout brings text and illustration together so every point is easy to follow." Phil had the knack; he had remarkable visual intuition as to how a book should "look," should "flow," and should "work" to the benefit of both reader and author.

Long into the recesses of the night when he did his most complex work, he drew upon a deep well of resources that enabled the complex conversion of the joined written word and illustration to a seamless progression of text and color-plates. Yet, even as he served as each book's choirmaster, he was invisible.

Invisible? Phil Grushkin's work was invisible?

Only a few really knew: the author, the publisher's editorial and design staff, the printer and the bindery. Yet, if his work was not of such high quality and artistic achievement, the faults of that expression would be fully apparent and off-putting. But the miracle of his work is that while his designer's imprint was everywhere within, nothing he did was actually noticed by The Reader, that unknown soul, that nameless purchaser of the work at hand. With Phil's elegant touch, nothing stood out and clamored, "Here I am, Mr. Clever Designer." Everything was in keeping — his choice of type, his grids and placements, the full association of all the elements. Everything served a greater purpose. Everything worked together so The Reader noticed...nothing. And yet...everything.

The strengths of a Phil Grushkin-designed book were always three: a completely rendered and efficient content, the strongest portrayal of the author's scholarship, and the full beneficence of the publisher. In essence, a beautiful and profound book. A most curious ego-applied and yet ego-free achievement.

There are literally ten thousand books in Phil and Jean Grushkin's home in Englewood, NJ, many representing Phil's involvement with major publishers throughout the world. But Phil also collected hundreds of works by his designer and typographer contemporaries.

One was W.A. Dwiggins, and one particular Dwiggins book, which was on the center of its shelf in the Grushkin dining room in Englewood, NJ for a half century, was MSS, published in 1947 by the Typophiles. Reading it, you can almost see Phil — and his teacher, George Salter — nodding in agreement as Dwiggins spelled out their argument concerning bookmaking. Dwiggins believed the role of the designer was that of an engineer. "The structure that a [book designer] builds must perform in a practical way," he wrote. "That practicality is a result partly of intuition, but mostly of a rational study of the end to be served. "Your proper bookmaking artist," said Dwiggins, "is always half engineer. A sense of weights and stresses, of structural fitness, of the right handling of materials, is as much a part of that artist's equipment as an intuitive sense of rhythmic spaces and graceful lines. "To be concerned with the shapes of letters and pages is to work with ancient and fundamental material," Dwiggins concluded. "The qualities of letter forms and good books are the qualities of a classic time: order, simplicity, grace. To try and learn and repeat their excellence

is to put oneself under training in a most simple and severe
school."

Phil Grushkin's lifelong schooling in the arts was indeed both severe and simple. He believed in the sanctity and purity of purpose of a job — one must be finished before the next one was begun. He was, after all, a commercial artist, but one who took tremendous pride in seeing his works prominently displayed in bookstores and in homes and reviewed by popular magazines and great newspapers across the world.

But this commercial artist was also humbled by an even greater Artistic Master, and here again I call upon Dwiggins to assist with this meditation: "It is conceivable," wrote Dwiggins. "that all forms of letters are modifications or degenerations of pen forms. And the Suitable Motions of the Pen may be taken as a guide in our search for Grace."

Dwiggins' "Suitable Motions" was a theorem that Phil embraced but which also perplexed him all his days and what he most often spoke of to his students. It was Philip Grushkin's task to reveal that the movement of the pen — the complex yet so simple pressures exerted between the hand, the pen, and the paper — is an ineffable life force that is expressed in calligraphy and then by extension in typography and design, and — we can only hope in today's world — in computerized design.

Phil Grushkin was a husband of fifty-three years to librarian Jean Grushkin, a father to Paul, Jonas, and Dena, a grandfather to six, a colleague to hundreds in cities all over the globe, a friend to hundreds more still, and will be remembered as one of New York's greatest bookmaking teachers. His legacy is that of a consummate bookmaking engineer in the time of man when momentous books were being made. Philip Grushkin's works will continue to thrive on bookshelves in millions of homes the world over. He leaves us admiring his gift. Thus, his work lives on forever — like the designers and calligraphers, painters and sculptors to whom he felt so closely matched — in timeless accomplishment.

Essay by Paul Grushkin (Philip's eldest son)

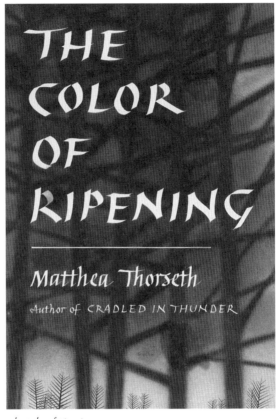

The Color of Ripening
By Matthea Thorseth. Superior Books.
Dust jacket with calligraphy and air-brush artwork by PG.

Taking Pen to Paper!

A calligraphic experience. Written out by PG [date unknown].

The Art of the Book

Slide lecture at the Englewood Library, Englewood, NJ by PG. Poster for the event designed and written by PG with added comments by the lecturer.

General Douglas MacArthur quoted from the poem "Youth" by Samuel Ullman.

Calligraphy by PG [date unknown].

A Quiet Place to Work

A novel by Harry Brown, Knopf [date unknown, about 1966].

Last book jacket designed by George Salter; rendered for reproduction by PG.

It was George Salter who opened up the doors to the book design and production field for Philip Grushkin. Phil, former student of Salter's, longtime friend, and for many years their mutual close friendship was like father-son relationship.

Happy Holidays – Pincus Family

Printed by PG on his CapGee Press.

A yearly chore Phil undertook with great joy. The family's "Thank you" attests to their appreciation.

Season's Greetings!

Each holiday season, Phil looked forward to designing (often with calligraphic overtones) cards for his family. His son Paul's participated in the very early ones.

The Cooper Union Art School Exhibition
(CUAS)

The Ninety-Eighth Annual Showing [date unknown].
Logo calligraphy by PG

Philip Grushkin's Logo (Monogram)

Spontaneity perhaps is one way to view Phil's logo —
created with the joy of the pen — the playfulness of the pen.
The logo dances across the page with unlimited freedom.

Marianne Moore "75"

Philip's "75" is used on the cover of a catalog published
for the American Academy of Arts and Letters on the
occasion of an exhibition in honor of Marianne Moore's
75th birthday. This lettering was originally made for
Grolier 75 [1959].
Printed by The Spiral Press, New York.

Originality In Books (essay)

Written out by PG, 1950. Calligraphy for a section in
"Bouquet for BR," published by The Typophiles in honor
of Bruce Rogers.

Contemporary Jewish Record

The American Jewish Committee, New York
Lettering for the masthead and stationery [date unknown]

The Shrine of the Word

An essay by Howard Mumford Jones sent with holiday
greetings, December 1967 from Ann and Joseph
Blumenthal, with decorations by PG, inscribed "With the
thanks of the printer to the decorator" respectfully Joe
Spiral (Joseph Blumenthal, printer).

Grolier 75: A biographical retrospective to celebrate the
Seventy-Fifth Anniversary of the Grolier Club in New York.

Designed and printed by Joseph Blumenthal at The Spiral
Press, New York. Title page numerals lettered by PG.

The Bulletin of the Marboro Book Club

Published by Marboro Book Club, Monthly Bulletin
Lettering for title page and subsequent pages by PG.

Book Find News: monthly bulletin

Published by the Book Find Club, New York.
Lettering for title page & subsequent page headings by PG.

Originality in Books

Until the Roman alphabet is superseded by some
different means of conveying thought, there is little
likelihood of any strikingly original development
in the making of either type or books. Perhaps the
designer of the future will be devoting his talent
to the decoration of phonograph records, or scrolls
such as the ancient Egyptians and Greeks and
Romans used. Some books are today actually transformed
into such records. Readers will become listeners.

Originality In Books (essay)
Written out by PG, 1950. Calligraphy for a section in "Bouquet for
BR," published by The Typophiles in honor of Bruce Rogers.

Trade Mark
Design by PG for Steuben Glass.

Seven Arts News

Published by Seven Arts Book Society, monthly bulletin.
Lettering for title page & subsequent page headings by PG.

Catalogue 26

Science, Medicine, Natural History, Bibliography and
Fine Printing.
Jonathan A. Hill, New York, 1985. Cover design by PG.

Catalogue 51

Science, Medicine, Natural History, Bibliography and
Fine Printing.
Jonathan A. Hill, New York, 1990. Cover design by PG.

Abrams Art Books

1962 Catalogue of Publications, Harry N. Abrams, Inc.
Lettering for the cover and subsequent pages by PG.

Christmas Carols

Oxford University Press, New York, 1948.
Designed by John Begg with calligraphy and music lettered by PG.

Publisher's Weekly The American Book Trade Journal

Masthead by PG.

Logo for Albert D. Smith & Co., Inc.

Rough drafts playing with the concept. Final use on company stationery, 1966–1970.

Logo designed for Joseph Bancroft & Sons, Co.

Some preliminary sketches, and final design on stationery,
and book cloth labels, 1963.
Design by PG.

Trade Marks

Design by PG for Steuben Glass, Knopf / Philip Grushkin
personal logo / sketch of a logo for Jean Grushkin.

Ani Maamin

A Song Lost and Found Again by Elie Wiesel.
Original lettering for jacket by PG.

CATALOG 26

MOSTLY RECENT

ACQUISITIONS

IN SCIENCE,

MEDICINE, AND

NATURAL HISTORY

JONATHAN A. HILL

NEW YORK 1985

Catalogue 26
Science, Medicine, Natural History, Bibliography and Fine Printing.
Jonathan A. Hill, New York, 1985. Cover design by PG.

Cooper Union Art School logo
Calligraphy by PG, circa 1950.

Cooper Union Art School Invitation

For the art school council to meet President and Mrs.
Burdell, 1950–1960. Calligraphy by PG.

Frege: Philosophy of Language by Michael Dummett

Dust jacket from original calligraphy by PG.

The Year at a Glance. Calendar 1942

Designed by Philip Grushkin for the Bauer Type
Foundry, New York.
Preliminary sketches and final printed version.

Holiday Magazine, February 1947

A literary map of the United States, color cartography by
PG, pp.140-141.

Love Songs of Asia

Rendered by Powys Mathers
Alfred A. Knopf, New York, 1946.
Typography and binding design by W. A. Dwiggins.
Jacket Design by Philip Grushkin.

Fables of Aesop

Handwritten by Philip Grushkin.
The Scribe, Archway Press, New York, 1946.
One of a series of five books written entirely by hand by
different calligraphers.

Christmas Carols

Selected and Annotated by William H. Crawford
Designed by John Begg.
Calligraphy and music executed by Philip Grushkin.
Oxford University Press, New York, 1948.

Calligraphics: Hands & Forms

Rendered by twenty-five American scribes for the
Typophiles, New York, 1955.
A collection of hand written pages, with "the Avant-Garde"
by Herschel Levit (pp.13–16) written out by PG.
Reproduced in one-quarter reduction from original writing.

The CapGee Press

He named it "The CapGee Press" (because the foot-pedal had a capital "G" on it)—an old eight-by-twelve Golding, clanked with a cap "G" treadle. He also obtained a large proofing press — all in the basement at 86 East Linden Avenue. Here Philip printed a host of season's greetings, family events (wedding and birth announcements, family visits, and occasional printings for grandchildren and friends). Phil collected some of his favorite type; his most favorite "Delphin."

Philip Grushkin, Chief Clanker, at 86 E. Linden Avenue, Englewood, NJ 07631.

Typeface Design

Experimental typeface design, never produced, circa 1955.

Typeface Design

[Untitled]

This book was hand bound, with calligraphy and illustrations by Philip Grushkin when he was a student at the Cooper Union, New York City in the 1940s.

His first attempt at hand-binding. Later, throughout his professional career he hand-bound books for presentation at the request of book publishers.

George Salter: A Third of a Century of Graphic Work,

Gallery 303, sponsored by the Composing Room, Inc., December 1961, New York.

Catalog designed by PG for an exhibition which contained thirty-four years of the graphic work of George Salter in Germany and in the United States. The show was organized by Meyer Miller for Gallery 303.

A History of Far Eastern Art

By Sherman E. Lee, Director, and Curator of Oriental Art, The Cleveland Museum of Art.

Harry N. Abrams, Inc. Publishers, New York, 1964.

Key Monuments of the History of Architecture

Edited by Henry A. Millon
Essays by Alfred Frazer
Harry N. Abrams, Inc. Publishers New York, 1965.
Designed by Philip Grushkin and Rose Lewis.

History of Art: A Survey of the Major Visual Arts from the Dawn of History to the Present Day

By H. W. Janson with Dora Jane Janson
Harry N. Abrams, Inc. Publishers, New York, 1966.
This book has gone through at least five editions and more than eight printings. It is considered the definitive text for art history courses.

History of Modern Art: Painting·Sculpture·Architecture

By H. H. Arnason
Vice President, Art Administration, The Solomon R. Guggenheim Foundation, 1968.

Thrice Told Tales: Folktales From Three Continents
Illustrated by Fritz Kredel
Edited by Kenneth S. Goldstein and Dan Ben-Amos
Privately published by Hammermill Paper Company,
Lock Haren, PA, 1970.

Raphael Soyer
By Lloyd & Goodrich
Harry N. Abrams, Inc. Publishers, New York, 1972.

American Chairs
Queen Anne and Chippendale by John T. Kirk
Alfred A. Knopf, New York , 1972.
Typography, binding & jacket design by Philip Grushkin.

The Legend of John Brown: A Biography and a History
By Richard O. Boyer
Alfred A. Knopf, New York, 1973.
Jacket and book design by Philip Grushkin.

Ani Maamin: A Song Lost and Found Again
By Elie Wiesel
Music for the Cantata composed by Darius Milhaud
Translated from the French by Marion Wiesel
Random House, New York, 1973.
Jacket design by Philip Grushkin, with lettering on title
page ("Ani Maamin") by Philip Grushkin.

Happy Times
Text by Brendan Gill. Photographs by Jerome Zirbe
Harcourt Brace Jovanovich, Inc., New York, 1973.

In the Minds and Hearts of the People
Prologue to the American Revolution 1760–1774
New York Graphic Society, Greenwich, Connecticut, 1974.

The Power Broker: Robert Moses and The Fall of New York
By Robert A. Caro
Alfred A. Knopf, New York, 1974.

Classic Lines: A Gallery of the Great Thoroughbreds
Richard Stone Reeves/Patrick Robinson
Oxmoor House, Inc., Birmingham, 1975.

'76 The World Turned Upside Down
By the Associated Press, 1975
Sid Moody

New York A Guide to the Metropolis. Walking Tours of Architecture and History
By Gerard R. Wolfe, New York University Press, 1975.

The Wild Gourmet: A Forager's Guide to the Finding and Cooking of Wild Foods
By Babette Brackett & MaryAnn Lash
David R. Godine, Publisher, Boston, 1975.

A Century of Champions
By the Associated Press Sports Staff, 1976
Supervising Editor: Ben Olan
Photo Editor: Thomas V. diLustro

Montpelier: The Recollections of Marion du Pont Scott as told to Gerald Strine
Charles Scribner's Sons, New York, 1976.

Your Show of Shows
By Ted Sennett
Macmillan Publishing Company, Inc., New York, 1977.

Vegetables Money Can't Buy But You Can Grow
By Nancy Bubel
David R. Godine, Boston, 1977.

Arboles de Buenos Aires
Silvina Ocampo/Aldo Sessa
Ediciones Libreria La Ciudad
Editorial Crea S. A., 1979.

The Spirit of the Enterprise
By Peter Mayer
Sixth of the R. R. Bowker Memorial Lectures New Series, 1979, R. R. Bowker Company, New York,
Booklet design by PG .

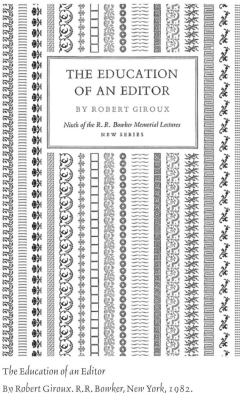

THE EDUCATION
OF AN EDITOR

BY ROBERT GIROUX

Ninth of the R. R. Bowker Memorial Lectures
NEW SERIES

The Education of an Editor
By Robert Giroux. R.R. Bowker, New York, 1982.

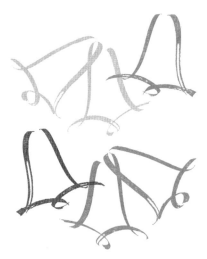

Decorations for personal Holiday Greeting card.

The Ghosts of Forever
By Ray Bradbury
Illustrations by Aldo Sessa
Rizzoli, New York, 1980.

Kennedy and Lincoln: Medical and Ballistic
Comparisons of Their Assassinations
By John K. Lattimer, MD, Sc.D., F.A.C.S., 1980.

The Sea Around Us by Rachel L. Carson
By Rachel Cartson
With an Introduction by Maitland A. Edey
Illustrated with photographs by Alfred Eisenstaedt
The Limited Editions Club, New York, 1980.

The Education of an Editor
By Robert Giroux
Ninth of the R. R. Bowker Memorial Lectures New Series,
December 16, 1981, R. R. Bowker Company, 1982, New
York. Booklet design by PG.

Mass Market Publishing – More Observations,
Speculations and Provocations
By Oscar Dystel
Eighth of the R. R. Bowker Memorial Lectures New Series
R. R. Bowker Company, New York, 1981.
Booklet design by PG.

The Mapping of America
By Seymour I. Schwartz and Ralph E. Ehrenberg
Harry N. Abrams, Inc., Publishers, New York, 1980.

John F. Kennedy Center for the Performing Arts
By Brendan Gill
Harry N. Abrams, Inc., Publishers, New York, 1981.

TVCVMAN
Fotografias. Aldo Sessa
Pulicado en la Argentina en 1982 por La GaceTa S.A.

Bibliography: Its History and Development
The Grolier Club, New York, 1984.
Bernard Breslauer and Roland Folter

Photographs by Hertha Bauer and Philip Grushkin
Set in Bembo type and printed letterpress at A. Colish, Inc.

A World History of Photography
By Naomi Rosenblum
Abbeville Press, New York, 1984.
The definitive text on the subject.

Impressionism and Post-Impressionism: The Hermitage, Leningrad, The Pushkin Museum of Fine Arts, Moscow and The National Gallery of Art, Washington
With introductions by Marina Bessonova and William James Williams.
Hugh Lauter Levin Associates, Inc., New York,
Aurora Art Publishers, Leningrad.
Distributed by Macmillan Publishing Company, New York, 1986.
Impressionism and Post-Impressionism was the result of a unique joint project completed by an American and Russian design team. This was the <u>first</u> joint publication to come out of the cultural exchange opened up by President Reagan and Premier Gorbachev in 1985.

Cellini
By John Pope-Hennessy
Principal Photography by David Finn
Additional Photography by Takashi Okamura and Others
Abbeville Press, Publishers New York, 1985.

The Art of Rock: Posters from Presley to Punk
By Paul D. Grushkin
Artworks photographed by Jon Sievert
Abbeville Press Publishers, New York, 1987.

Water Lilies
By Charles F. Stuckey
Hugh Lauter Levin Associates Inc., New York
Distributed by Macmillan Publishing Company, New York, 1988.

The Art of Florence
By Glenn Andres, John M. Hunisak, A. Richard Turner
Principal photographs by Takashi Okamura

Abbeville Press Publishers, New York, 1988.
2 volumes boxed.

The Carving of Mount Rushmore
By Rex Alan Smith
Abbeville Press, Publishers, New York, 1985.

Allies: Great U. S. and Russian World War II Photographs
Introductions by Grigori Chudakov and David E. Scherman
Hugh Lauter Levin Associates, Inc. New York.
Distributed by Macmillan Publishing Company, New
York, 1989.

Atlas of Human Anatomy
By Frank H. Netter, M. D.
Sharon Colacino, Ph.D, Consulting Editor
Ciba-Geigy Corporation, Summit, New Jersey, 1989.
The design of Dr. Frank Netter's book on Human
Anatomy was clearly the greatest challenge to Philip
Grushkin as a book designer. Dr. Netter's anatomical
drawings had to be reproduced with absolute accuracy
accompanied by precisely positioned leaders and captions.
For the book designer it also meant a handsome book, in
overall design. This book took at least two years to com-
plete. A classic text revered by doctors and medical students throughout the world.

Fabergé and the Russian Master Goldsmiths
Edited by Gerard Hill
Hugh Lauter Levin Associates, Inc.
Distributed by Macmillan Publishing Company, New
York, 1989.

Masterpieces of Japanese Screen Painting
Introductory Essay and Commentaries by Miyeko Murase
George Braziller, New York, 1990.
The many gatefold plates in large format made this book
another production challenge.

Medicine: A Treasury of Art and Literature edited by Ann
G. Carmichael and Richard M. Ratzah
Hugh Lauter Levin Associates, Inc., 1991.

Great Paintings of the Western World

By Alison Gallup, Gerhard Gruitrooy, and Elizabeth M.
Weisberg
Hugh Lauter Levin Associates, Inc. 1997.

Winslow Homer Watercolors

Nicolai Cikovsky, Jr.
Hugh Lauter Levin, Associates, Inc.
Distributed by Macmillan Publishing Company, New
York, 1991.

The Civil War: A Treasury of Art and Literature

Edited by Stephen W. Sears
Hugh Lauter Levin Associates, Inc.
Distributed by Macmillan Publishing Company, New
York, 1992.

Baseball: A Treasury of Art and Literature

Edited by Micahel Ruscoe
Hugh Lauter Levin Associates, Inc.
Distributed by Macmillan Publishing Company, New
York, 1993.

Space: Discovery and Exploration

Edited by Martin J. Collins and Sylviak K. Kraemer
Hugh Lauter Levin Associates, Inc., 1993.
Smithsonian Institution, National Air and Space
Museum.

The Western World

By Michael Ronnen Safdie
With an Introduction by Yehuda Amichai
Hugh Lauter Levin Associates, Inc., 1997.

Dissector for Netter's Atlas of Human Anatomy

Discussions Vol. II
by Sharon Oberg, Ph.D.
CIBA-GEIGY Corporation, Summit, New Jersey, 1994.
Design by Philip Grushkin.

Jewish Art
By Grace Cohen Grossman
Hugh Lauter Levin Associates, Inc., 1995.

Einstein's 1912 Manuscript on the Special Theory of Relativity: A Facsimile
George Braziller, Publishers in association with the Jacob
E. Safra Philanthropic Foundation and the Israel
Museum, Jerusalem, 1995.

Christmas Treasures
Edited by Deborah Cannarella
Hugh Lauter Levin Associates, Inc., 1998.

Battles of the Civil War: The Complete Kurz & Allison Prints 1861–1865
Oxmoor House, Inc., Birmingham, 1976.

Tropica: Color Cyclopedia of Exotic Plants and Trees from the Tropics and Subtropics for Warm-Region Horticulture–in Cool Climate, the Sheltered Indoors
By Alfred Byrd Graf, D. Sc.
Roehrs Company Publishers, East Rutherford, NJ, 1978.

Nevelson's World
By Jean Lipman
Hudson Hills Press, New York, 1983,
in association with the Whitney Museum of American Art.

Van Gogh: in Provence and Auvers
By Bogomila Welsh-Ovcharov
Hugh Lauter Levin Associates Inc., 1999.
The last book designed by Philip Grushkin. It was dedicated to the memory of Philip Grushkin by Hugh Lauter Levin.

Exhibition curated by Jean Grushkin, with assistance
from Dena Florczyk, Jonas Grushkin, and Paul Grushkin.
Typography and design by Jerry Kelly using Georg Trump's Delphin
typeface, which was Phil Grushkin's favorite font.